Puppies and kittens in the house, farm animals in the field and farmyard, and friendly creepy-crawlies in the garden – all the familiar animals a young child is likely to encounter are here delightfully illustrated. A charming book of first animal words for parents to say with their babies.

Edwina Riddell studied graphic design at the London College of Printing and worked for ten years as a freelance illustrator. Now, with two small children, her major interest is in children's books. She has illustrated **Outside In** and **See How You Grow,** both of which are lift-the-flap body books. **My First Animal Word Book** is a sequel to her extremely successful **100 First Words.**

for Max

My First Animal Word Book
© Frances Lincoln Limited 1989
Illustrations © Edwina Riddell 1989

My First Animal Word Book was conceived, edited and designed by
Frances Lincoln Limited, Apollo Works,
5 Charlton Kings Road, London NW5 2SB

ISBN   0-7112-0547-7 hardback
ISBN   0-7112-0546-9 paperback

9 8 7 6 5 4 3 2

Printed and bound in Hong Kong by Kwong Fat

Design and art direction Debbie MacKinnon

my first animal word book

Edwina Riddell

FRANCES LINCOLN

tail

Kitten

cat

basket

fur

claws

whiskers

bell

milk

ear

dog

tail

nose

lead

tongue

collar

puppy

paw

bone

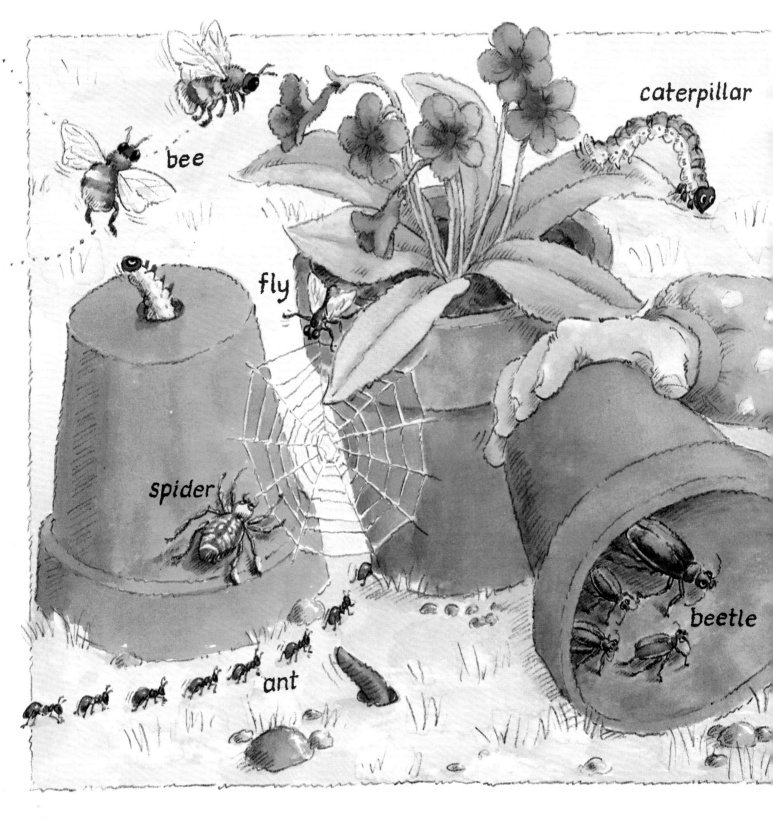

bee

caterpillar

fly

spider

ant

beetle

butterfly

ladybird

worm

snail

rabbit

guinea pig

tortoise

budgie

parrot

fish

tank

hamster

owl

beak

bird

squirrel

worm

wing

nest of
baby birds

swan

goslings

goose

tadpoles

frog

dragonfly

duck

ducklings

donkey

cow

hoof

calf

horse

mane

sheep

pig

mouse

piglets

cockerel

lamb

hen

chicks